THE OFFICIAL MINECRAFT COLOURING BOOK

Create, Explore, Relax

TITAN BOOKS

LONDON

Dear Adventurer,

You have spent countless hours mining, building, and exploring the Minecraft world and have honed your creative skills to epic proportions. So, after surviving a harrowing night of hostile mobs, it's time for you to sit back, relax, and use your imagination to colour something truly amazing. Inside the pages of this book, you will find familiar characters, mobs, blocks, weapons, armour, and biomes that can be shaped into works of Minecraft art—by you! Oh, Adventurer, your task will not be an easy one. You will encounter creeper attacks, a zombie horde, and even the Ender Dragon. Fear not, though—you have your trusty diamond sword and coloured pencils to fend off those hostile mobs. So, sharpen up your favourite weapons, engage your creativity, and bravely go colour without limits!

Sincerely,
The Guide

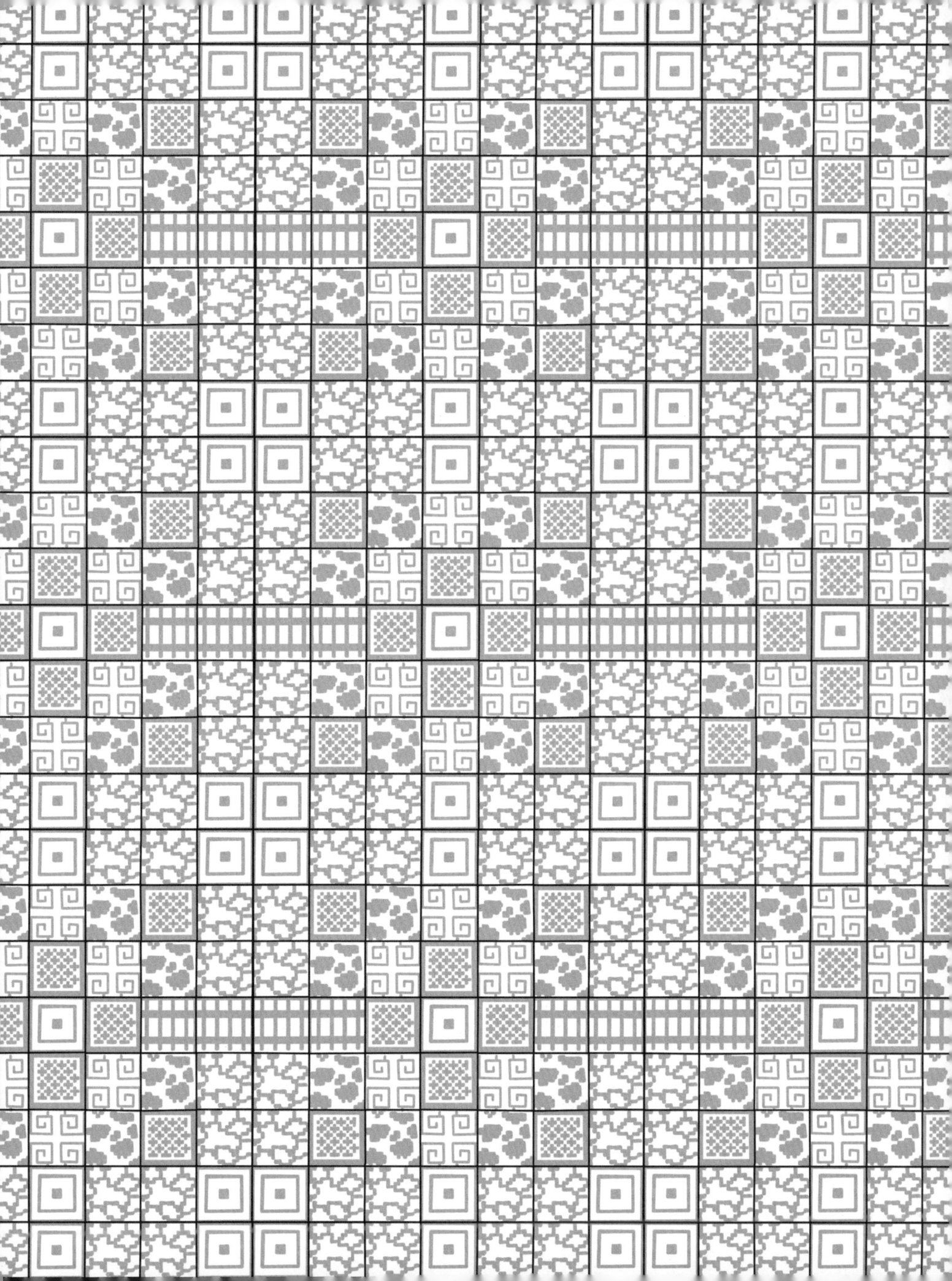

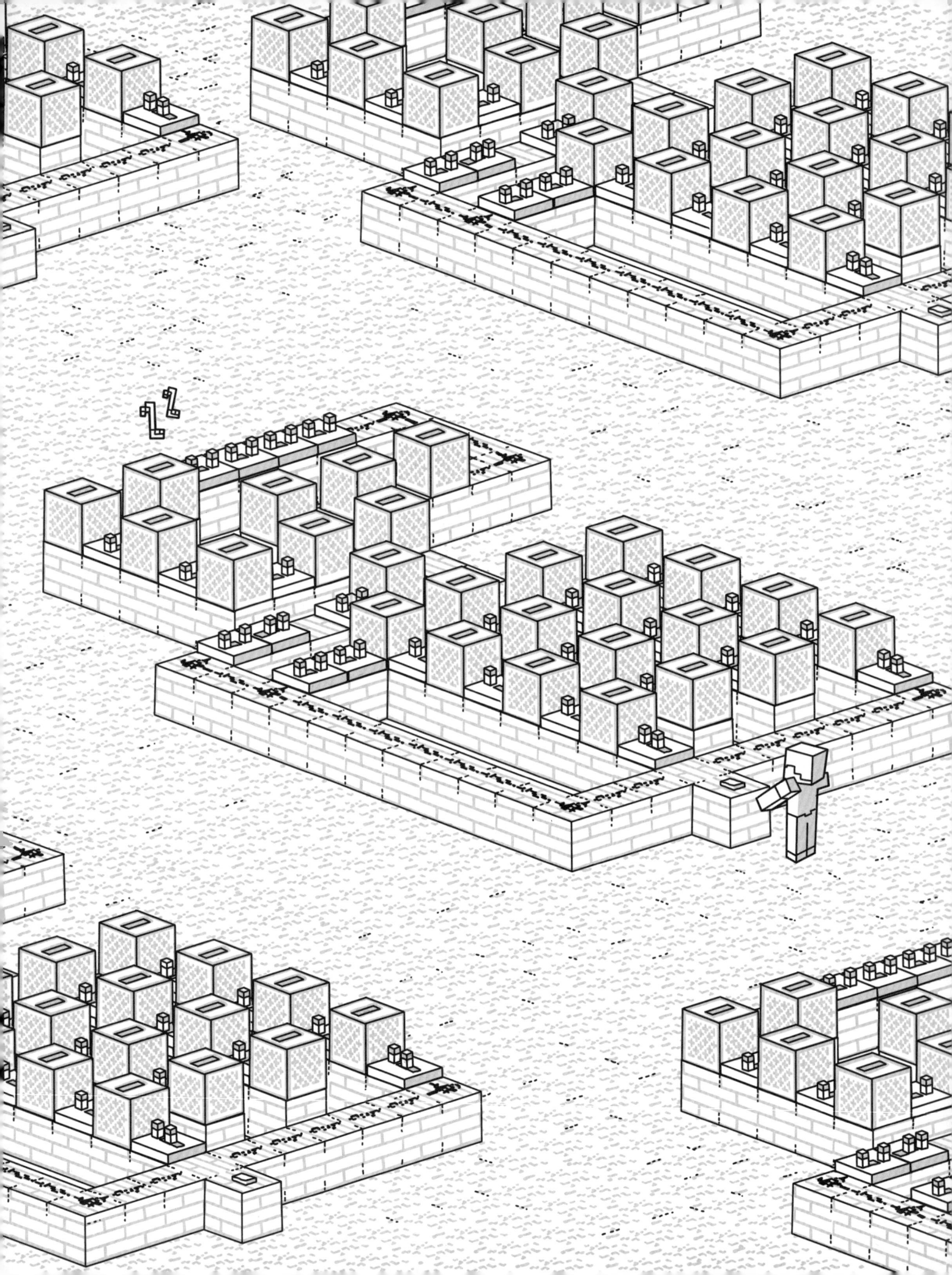

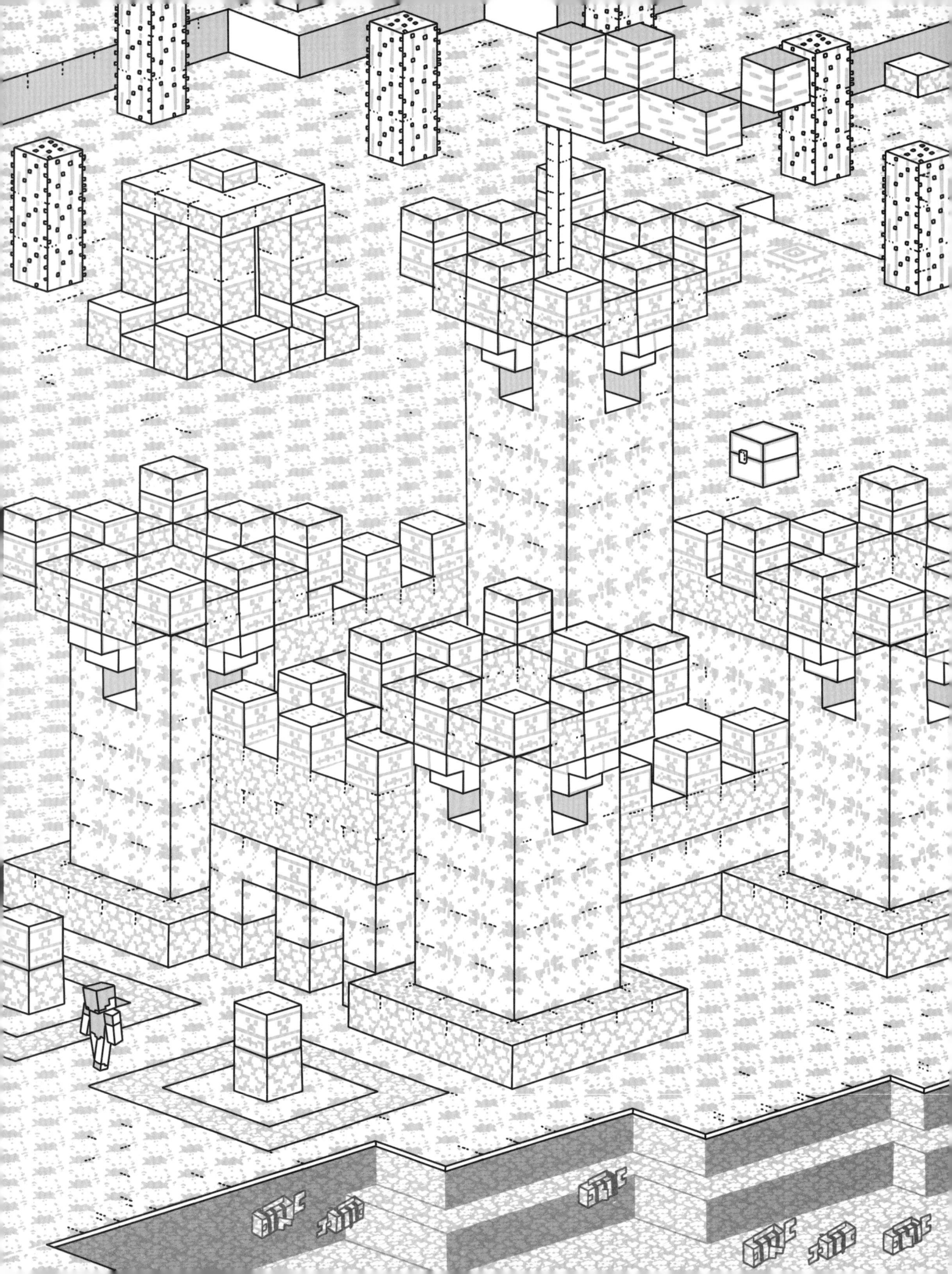

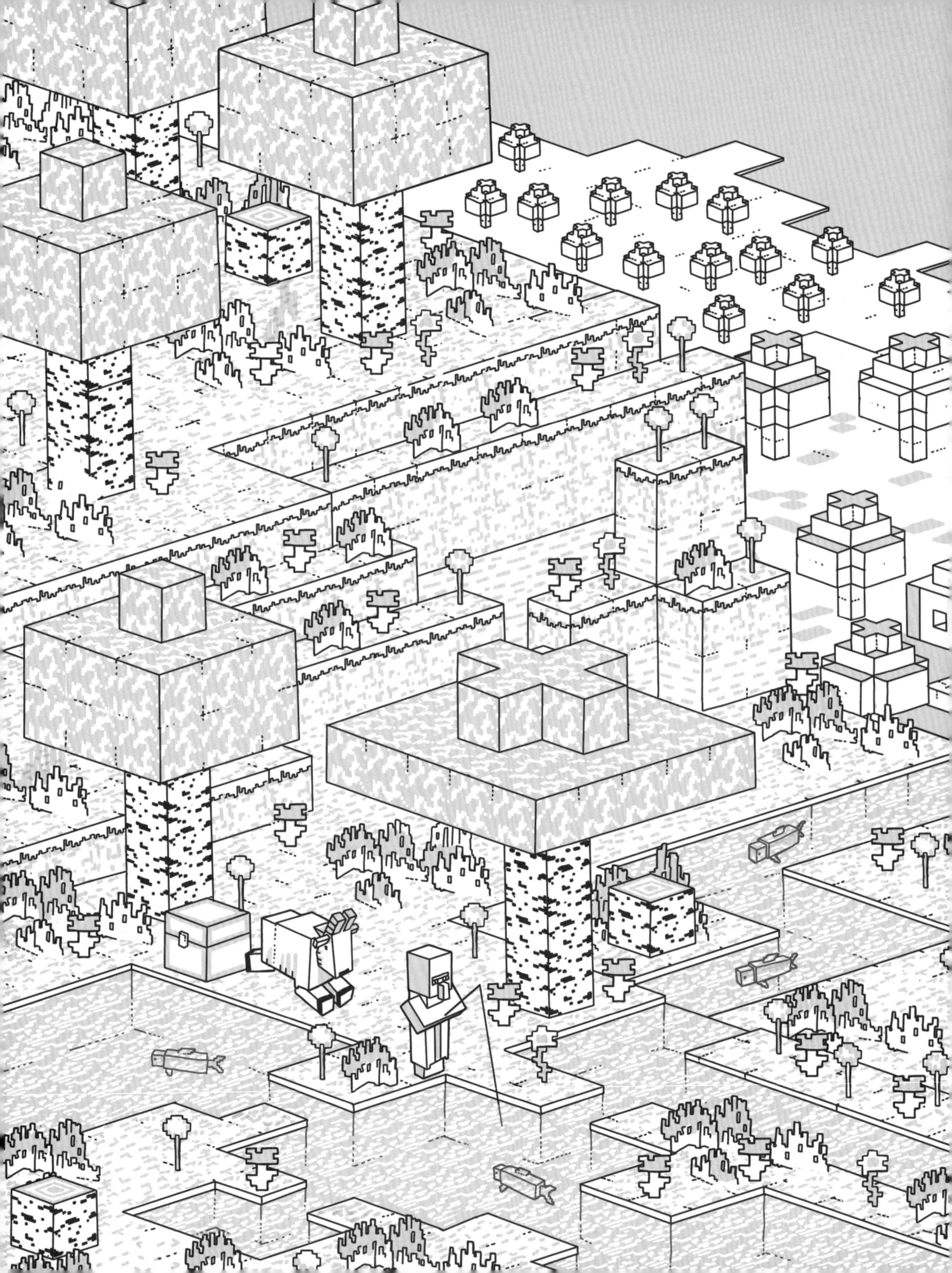

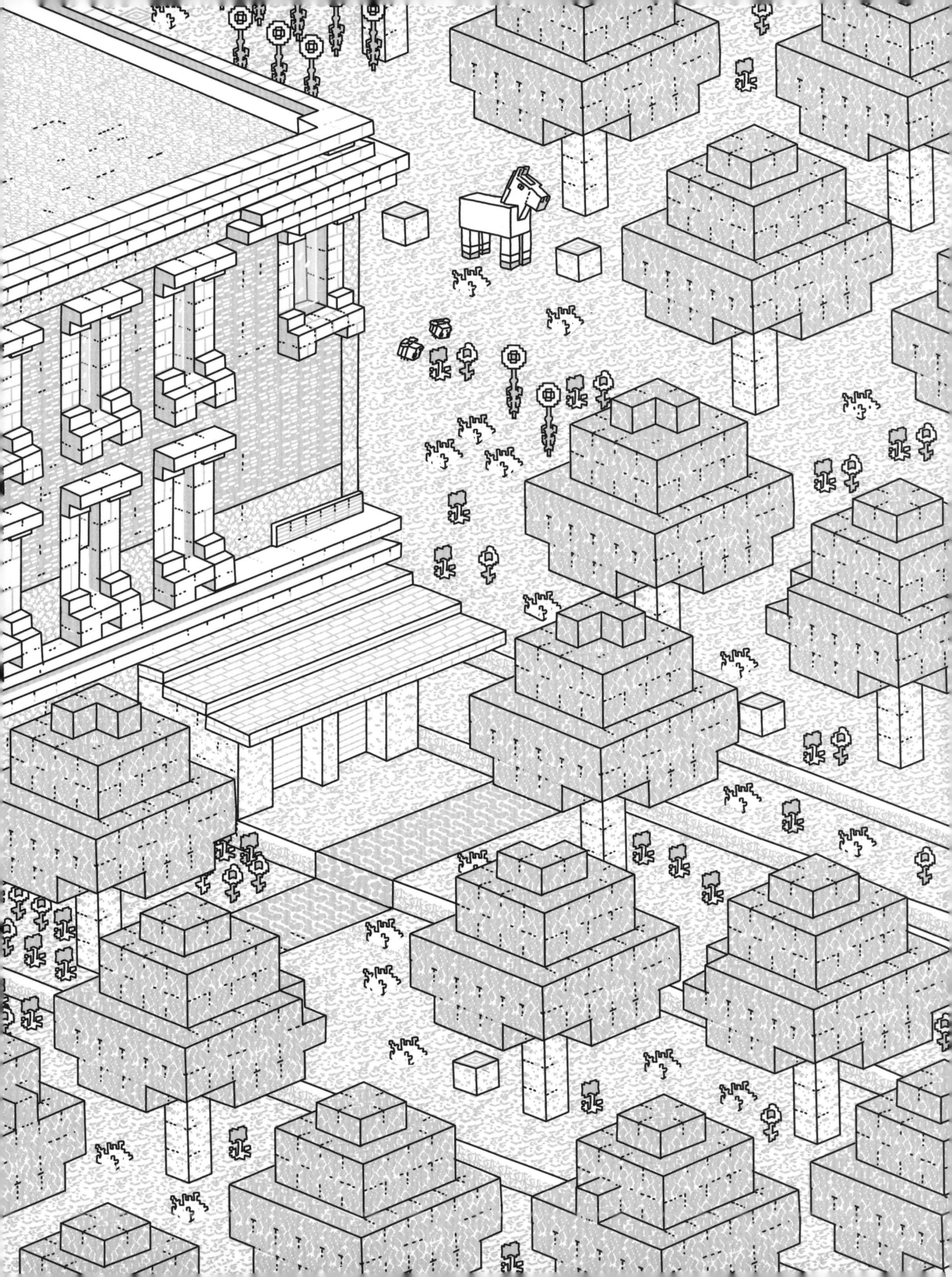

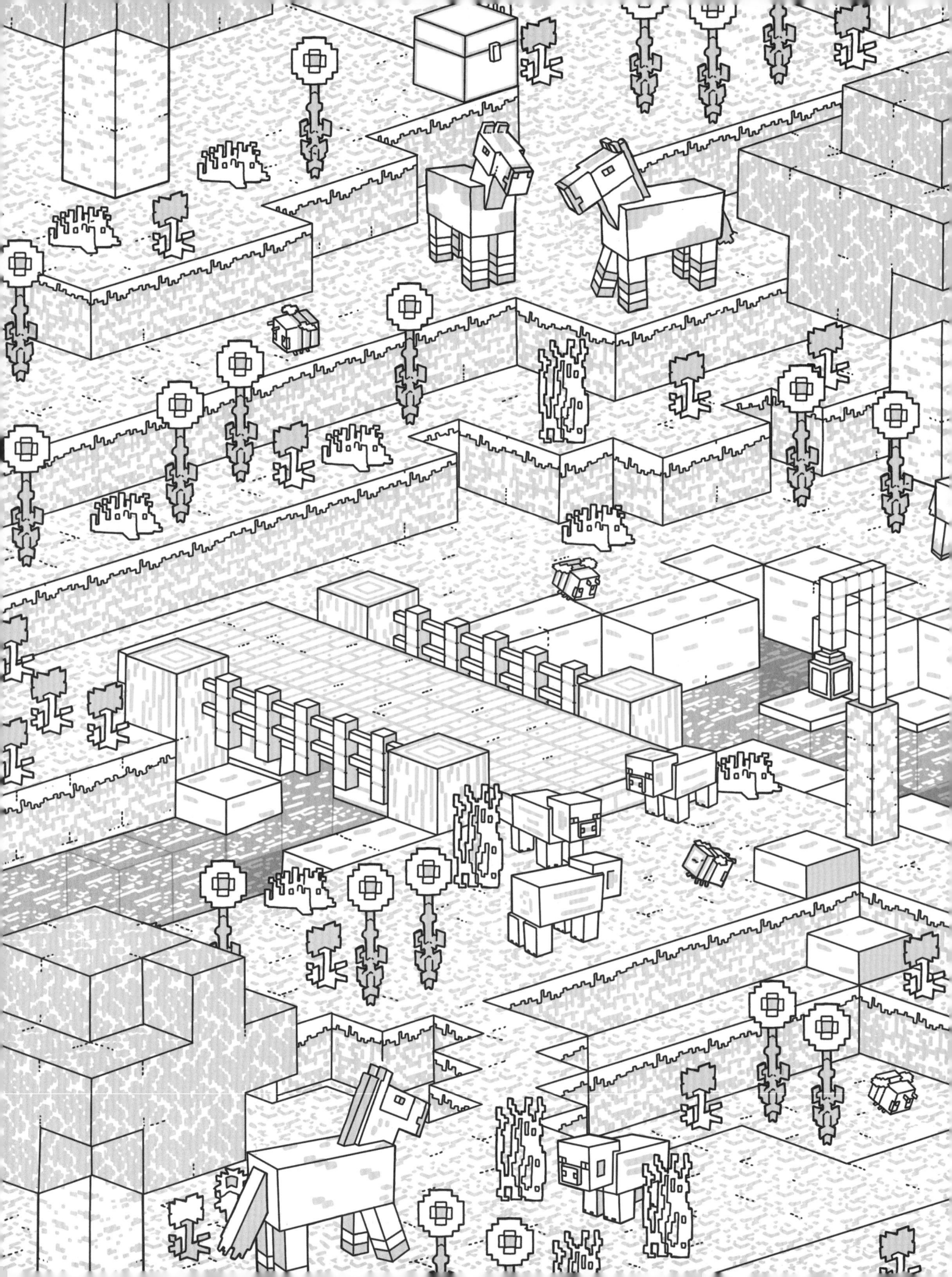

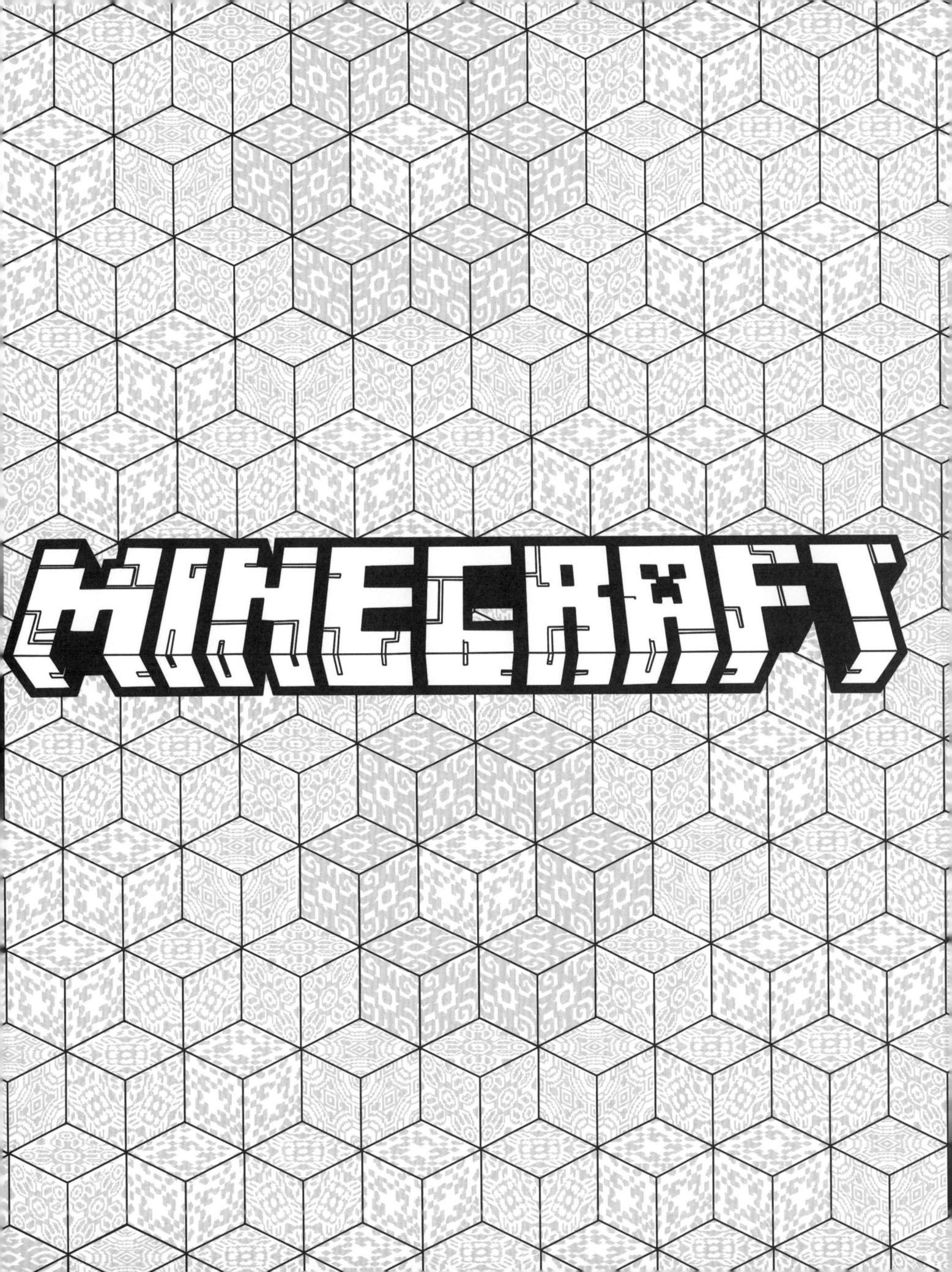

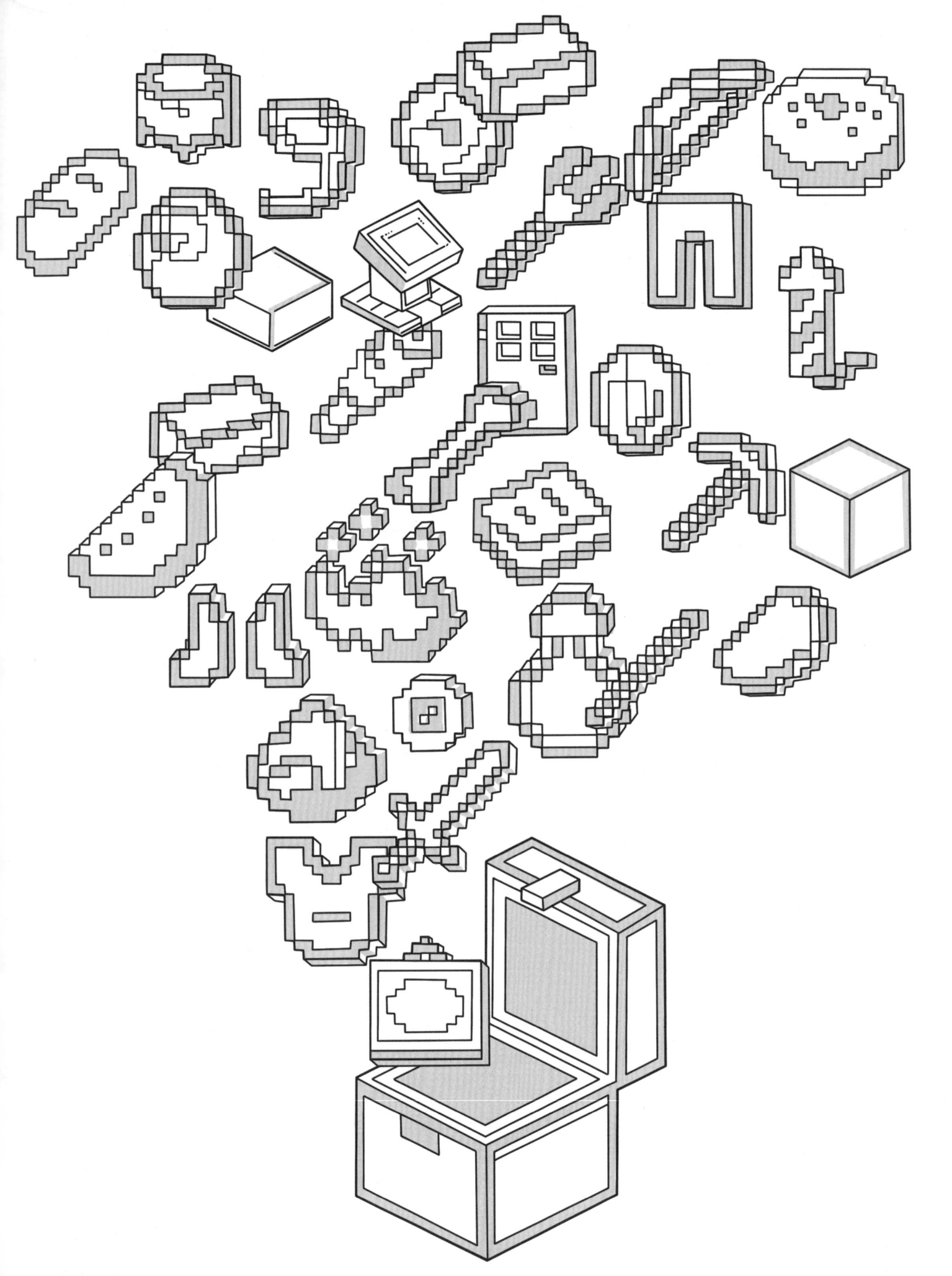

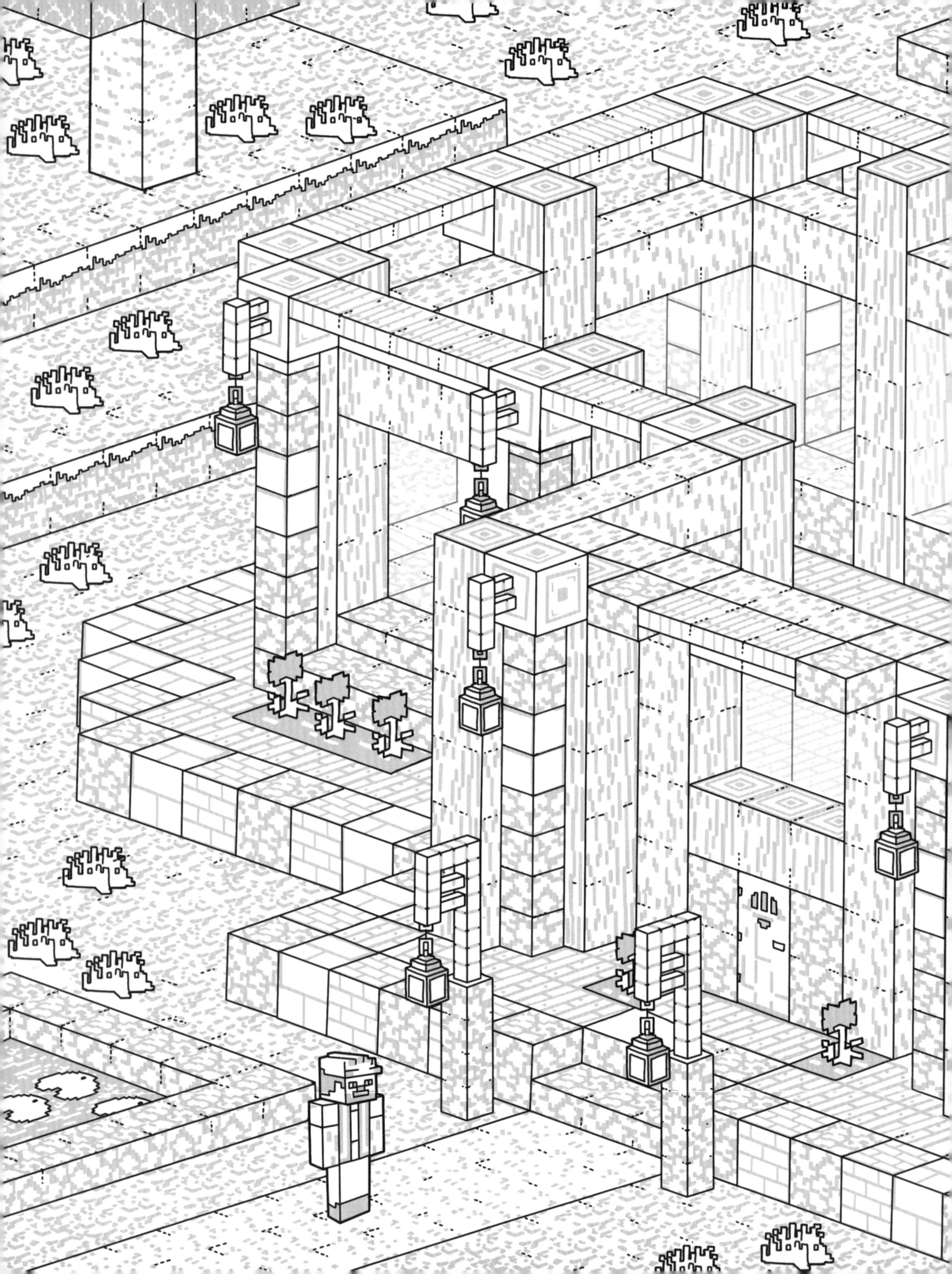

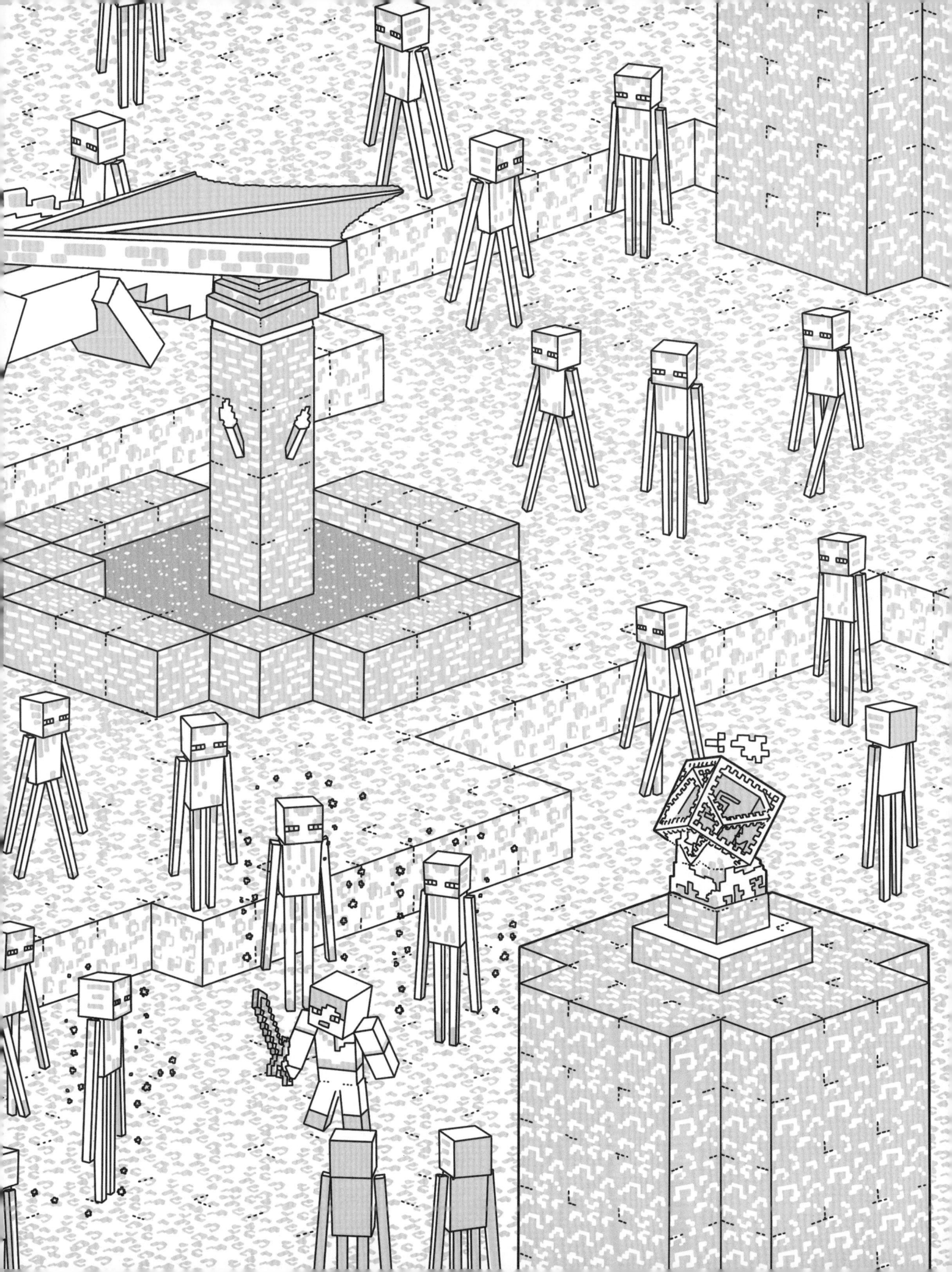

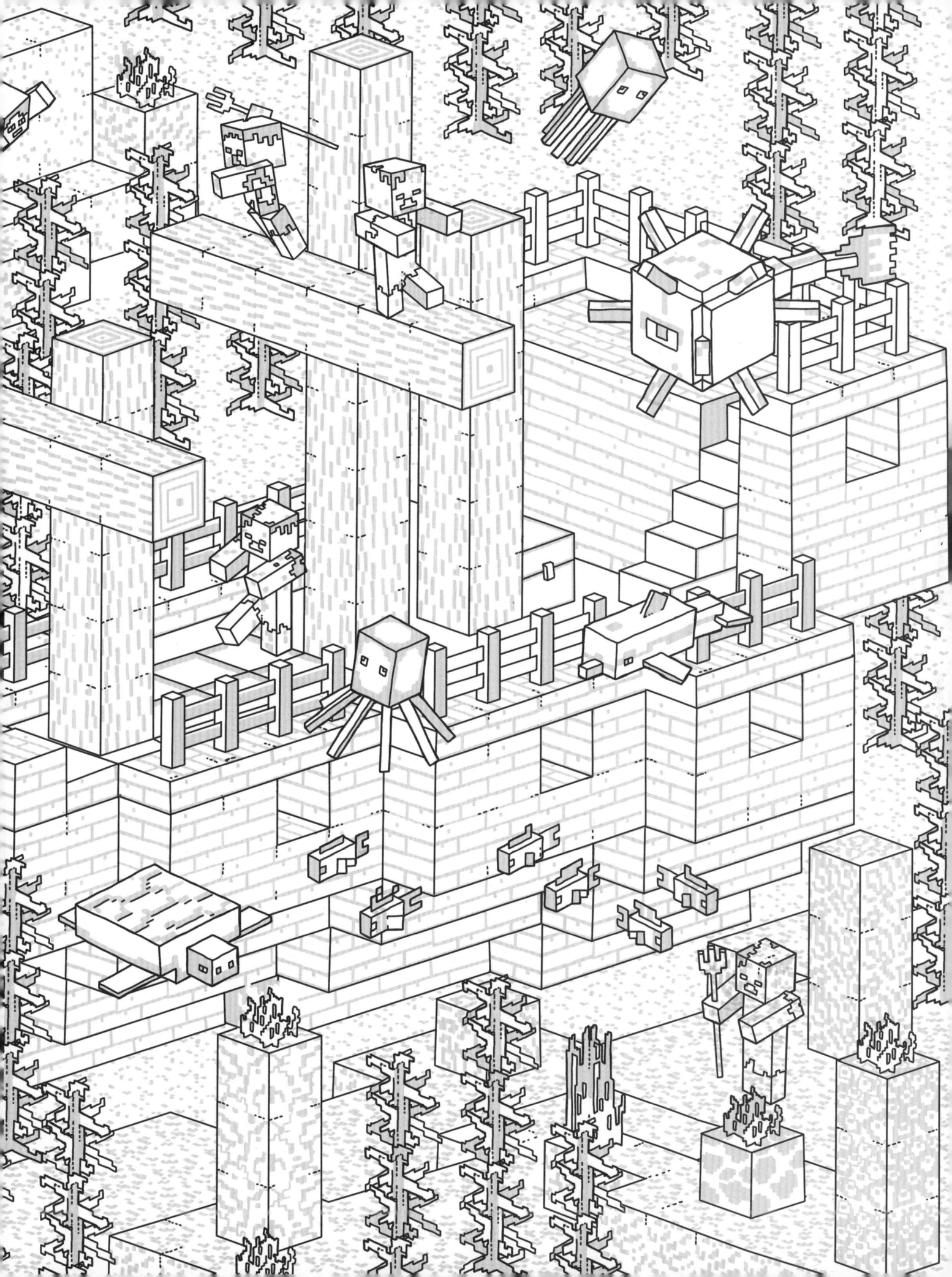

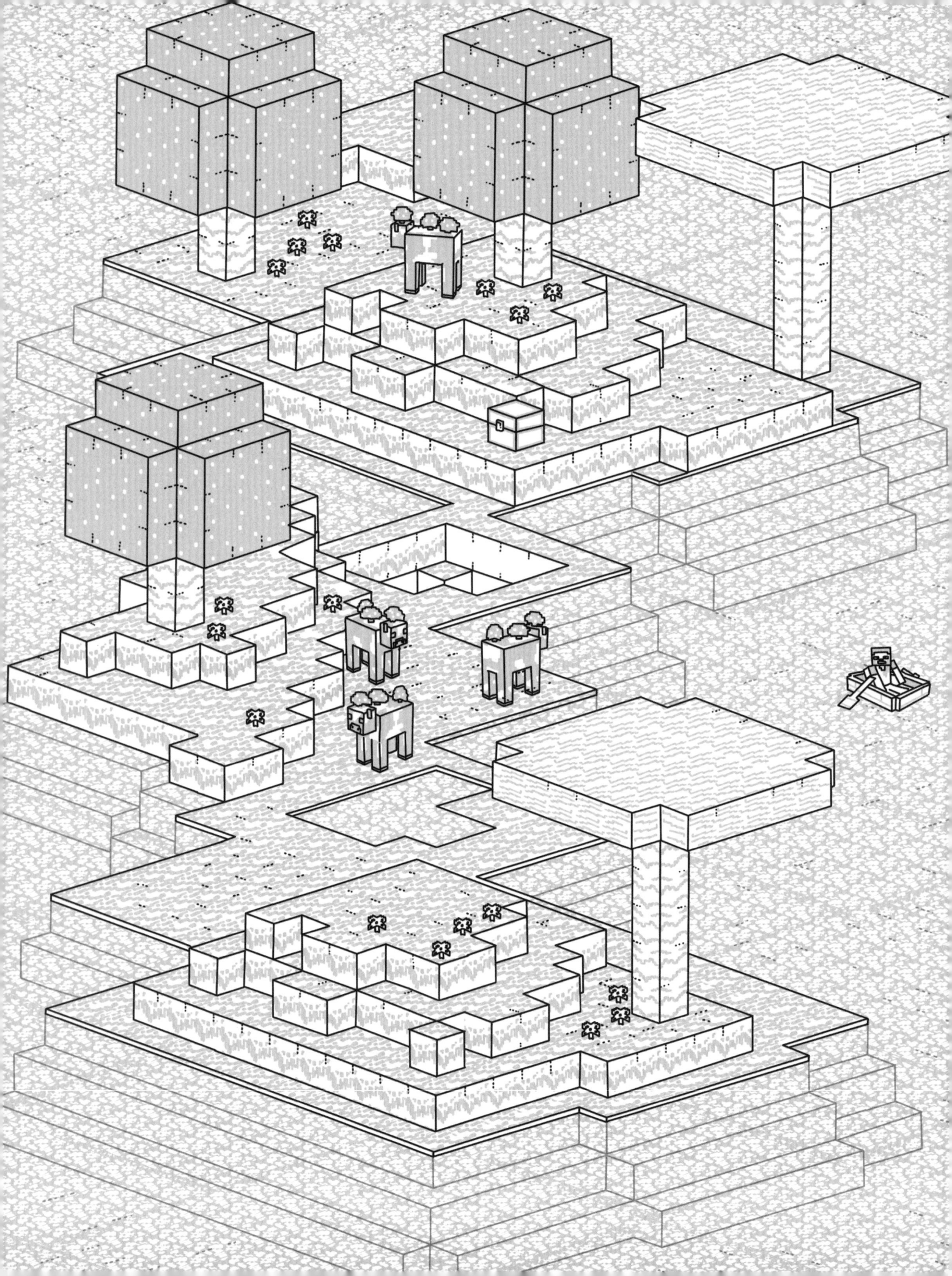

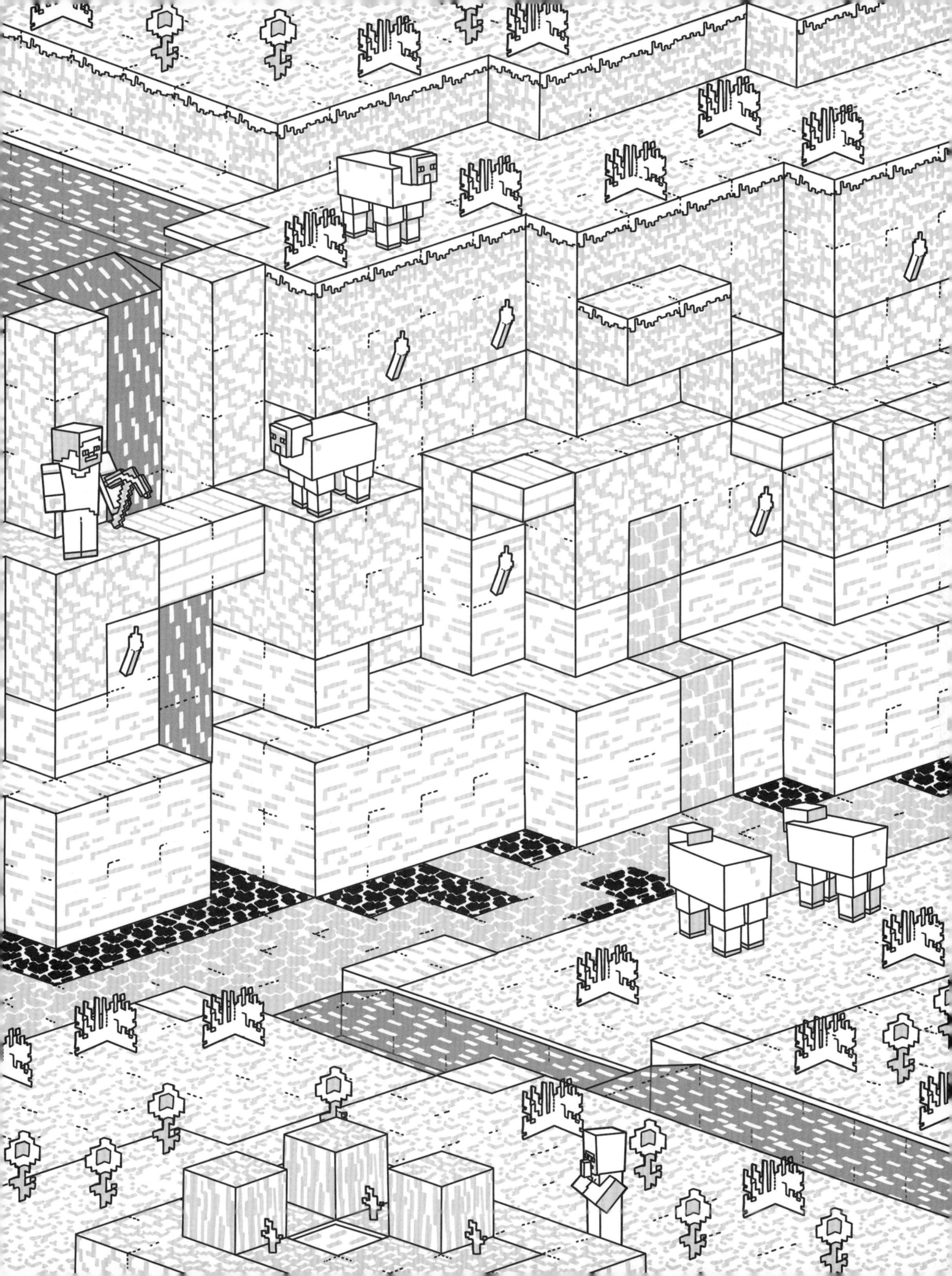

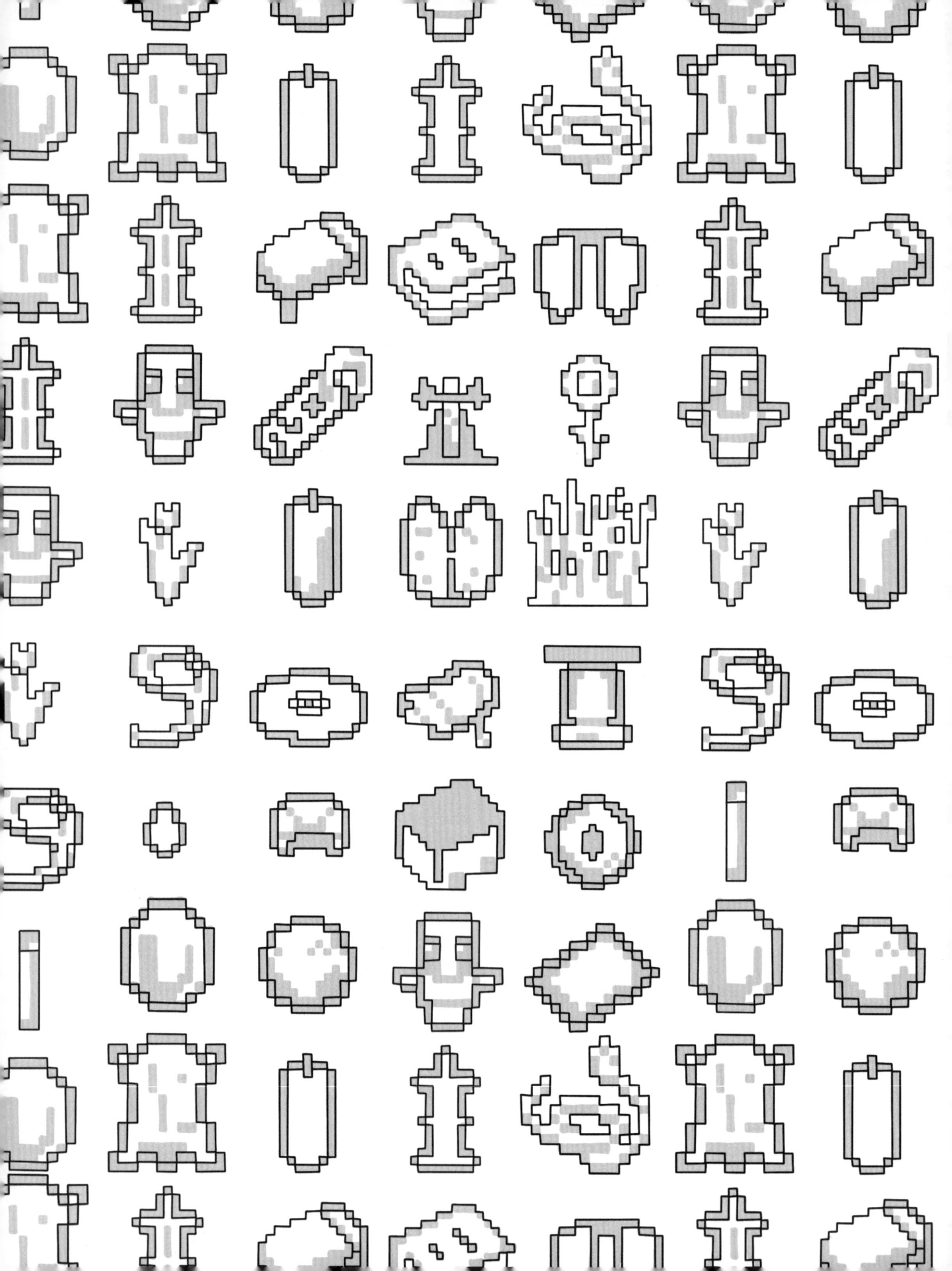

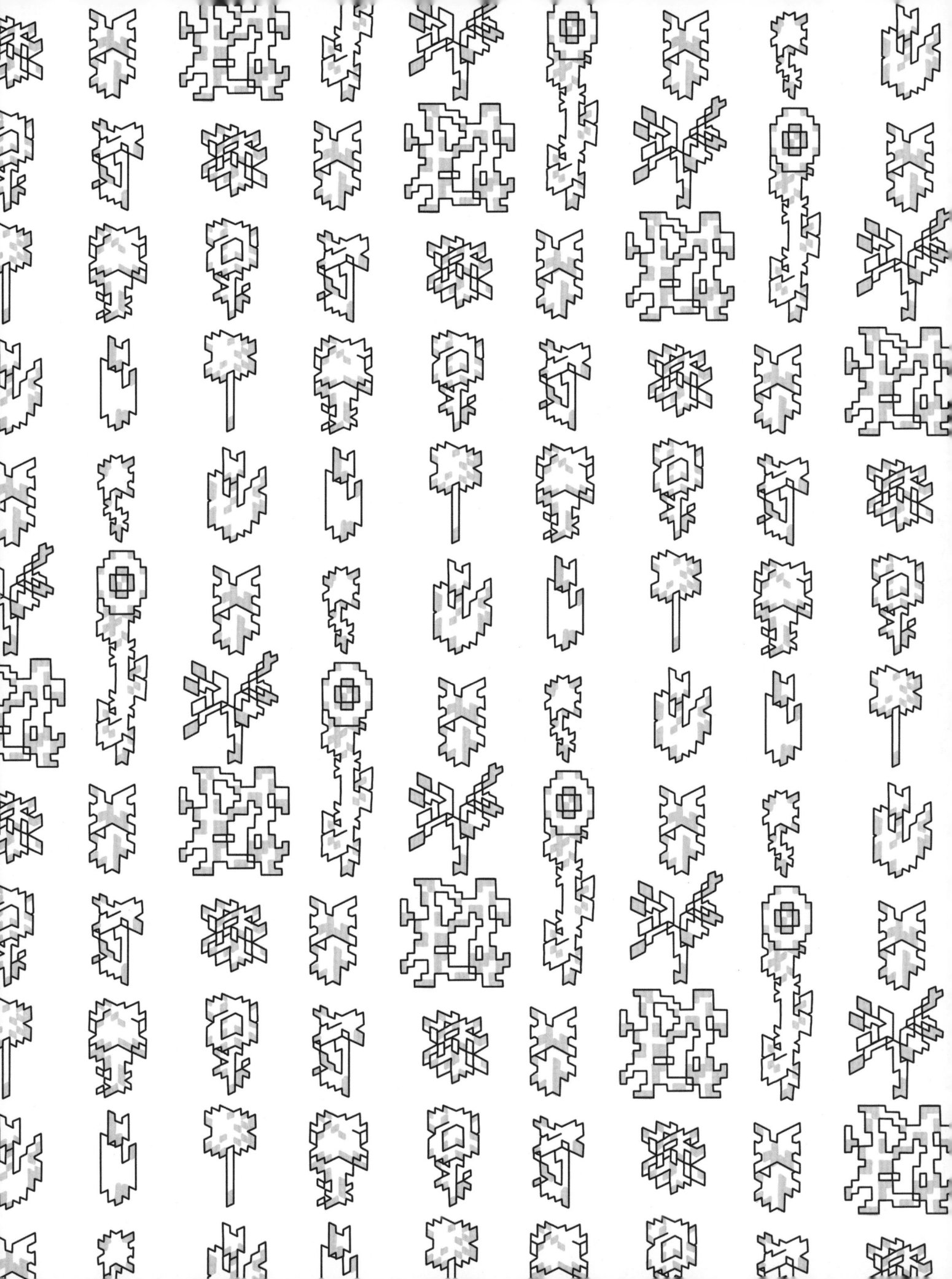

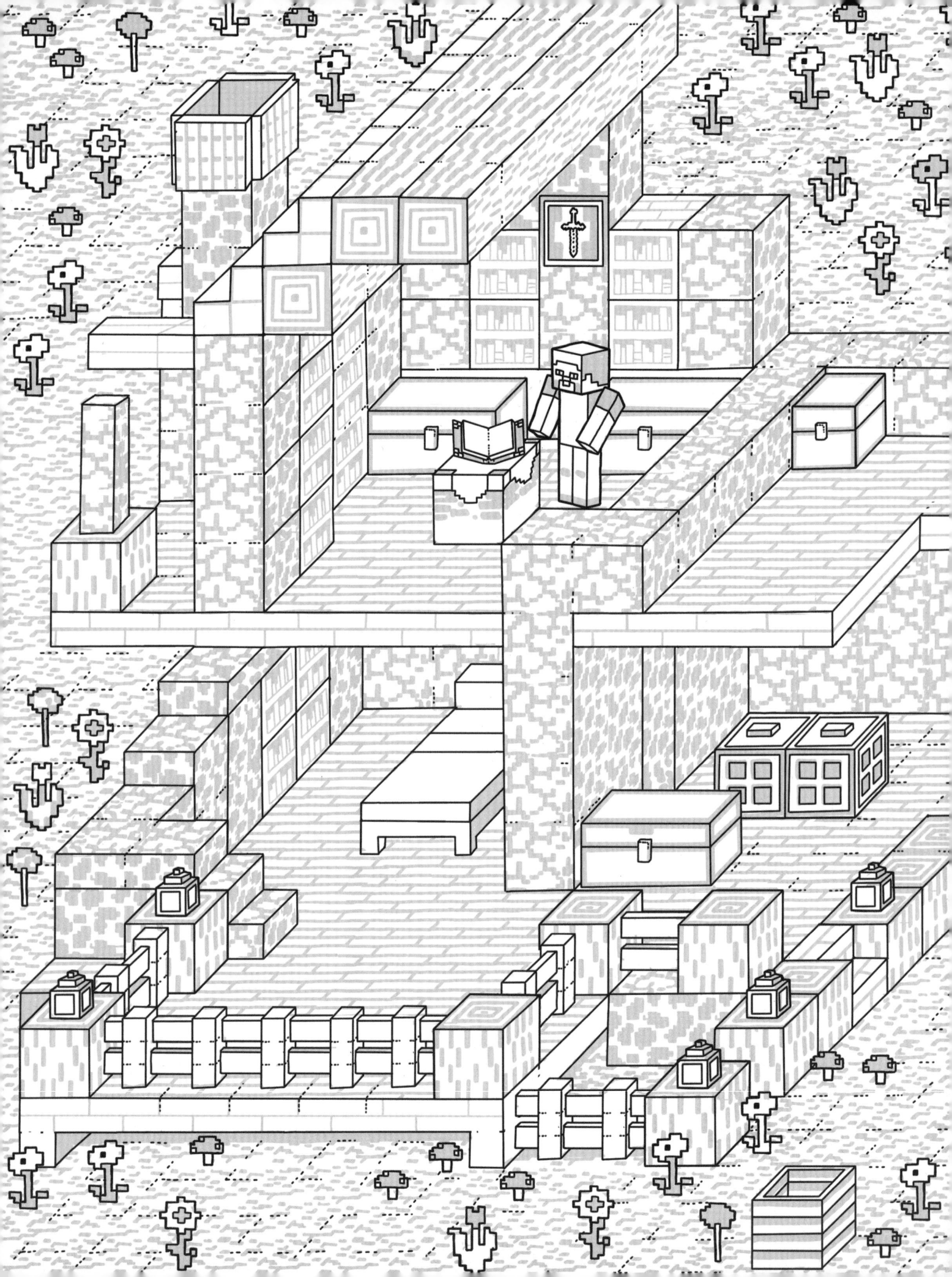

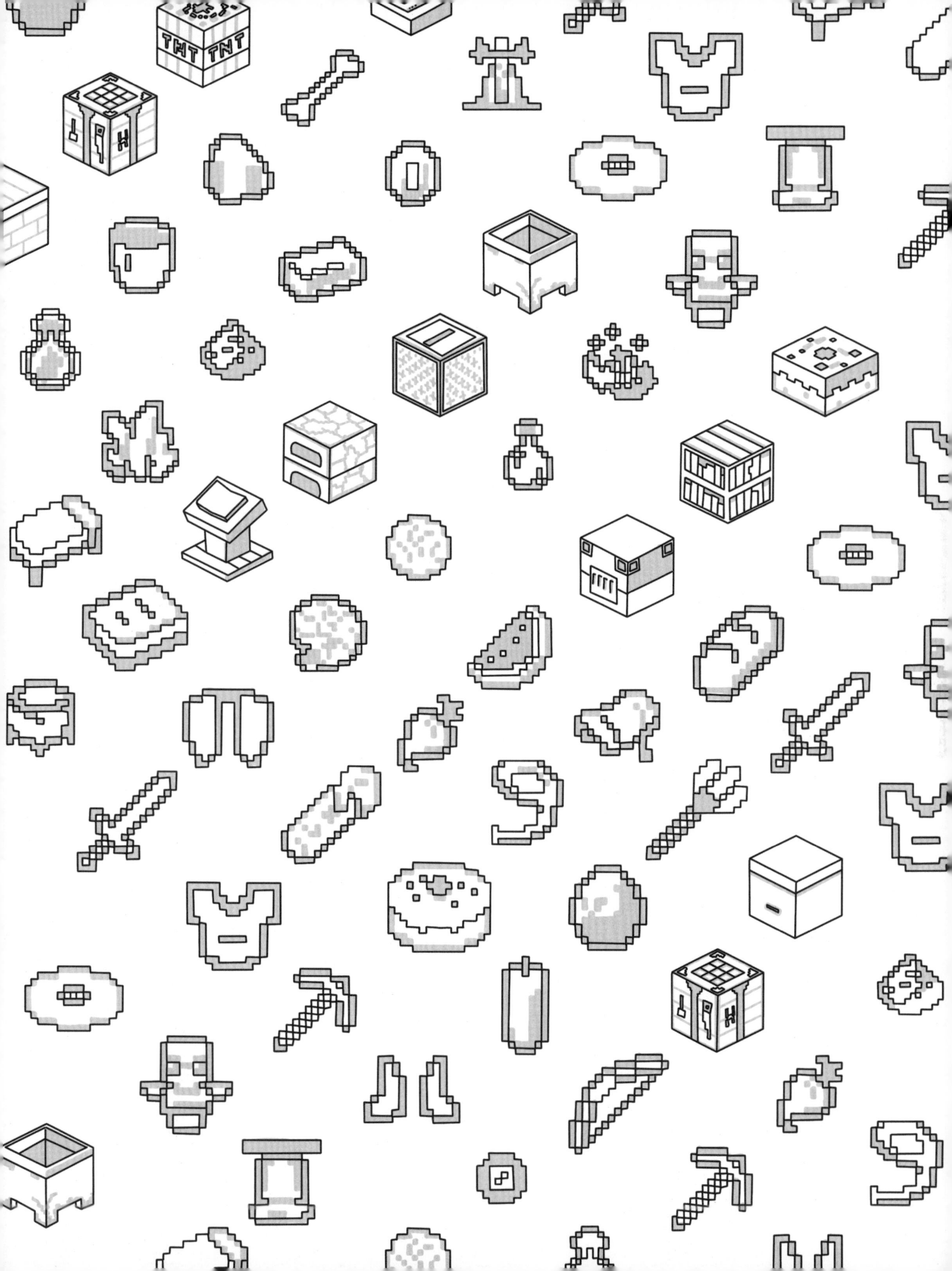

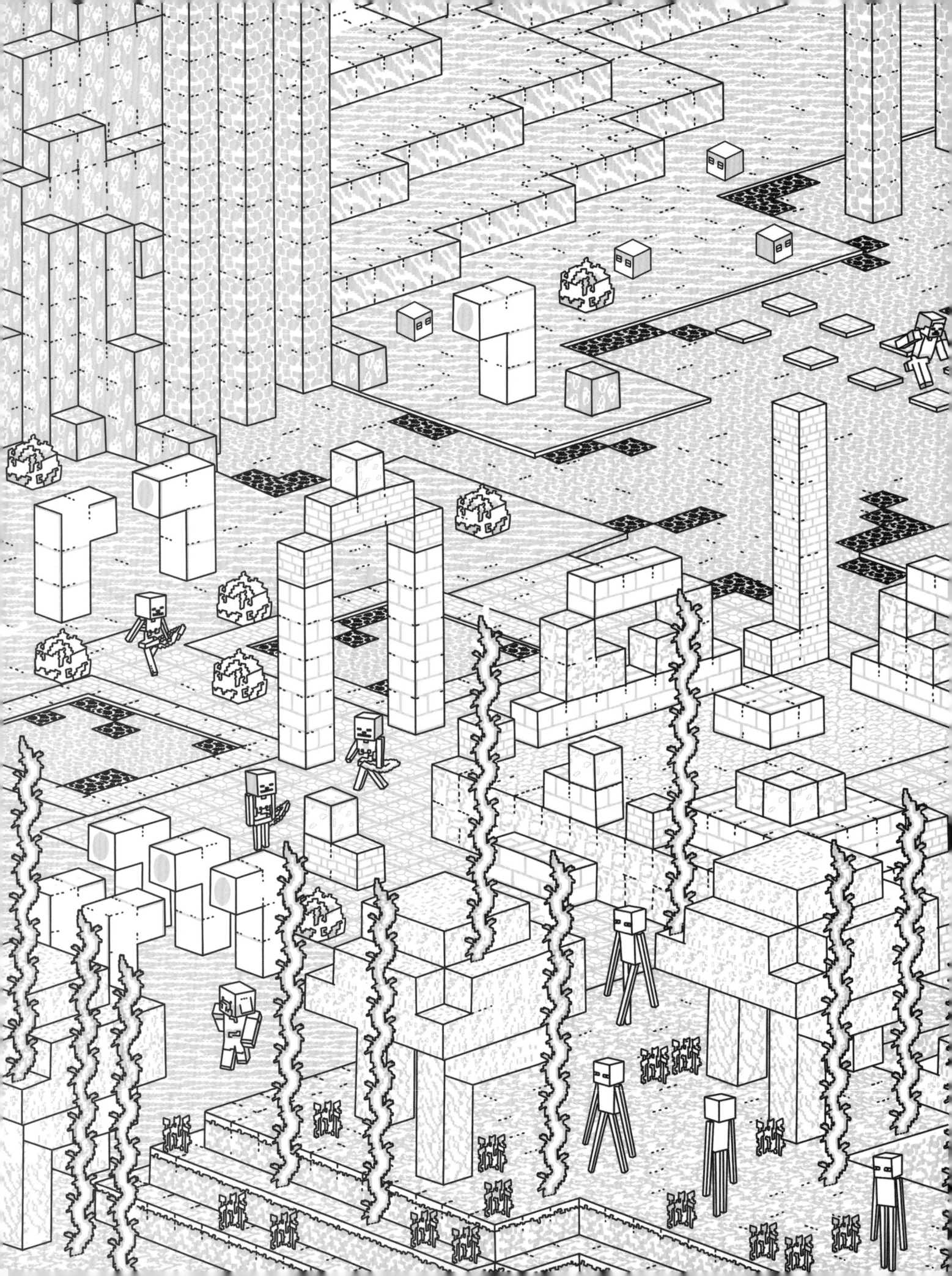

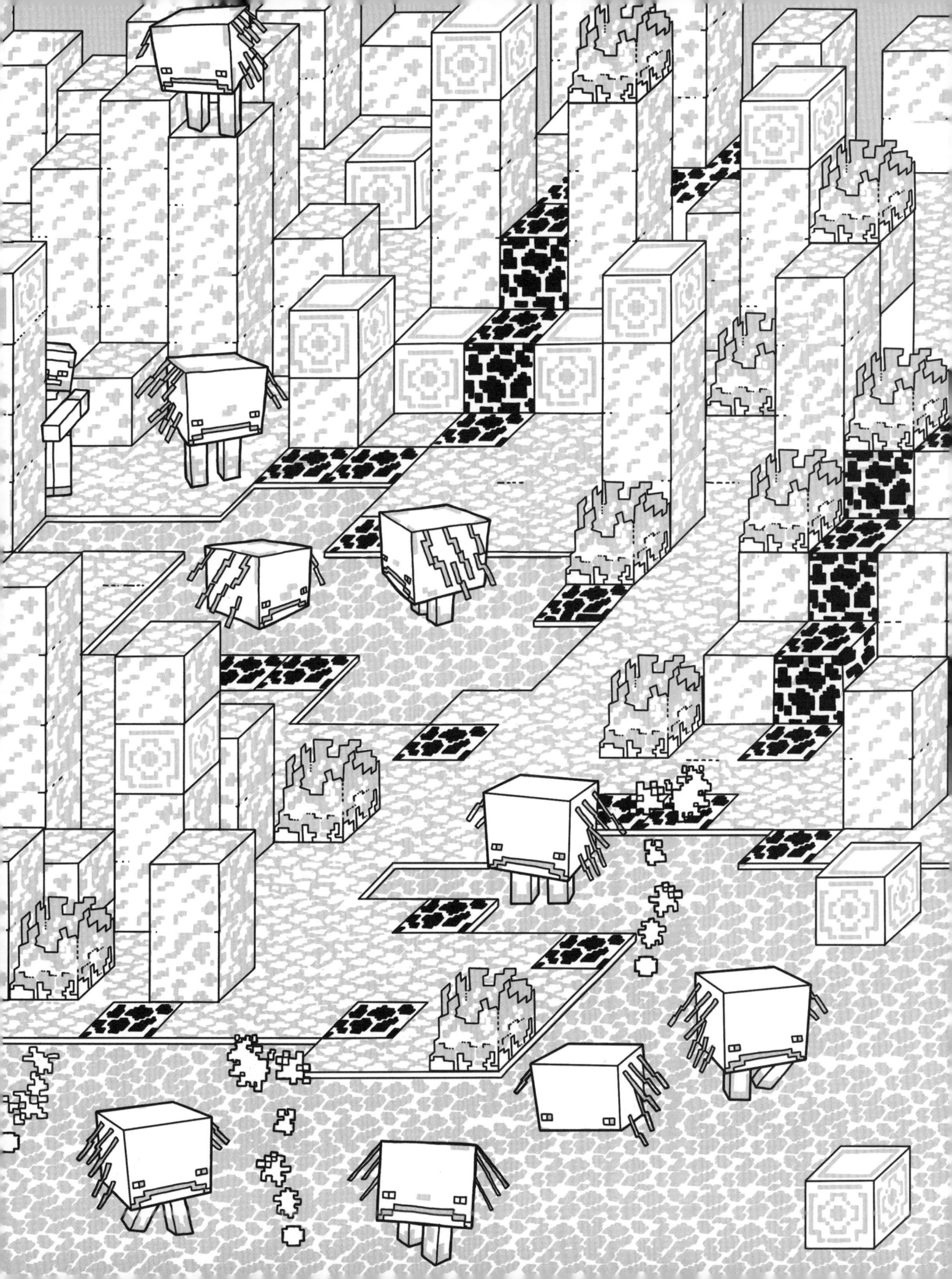

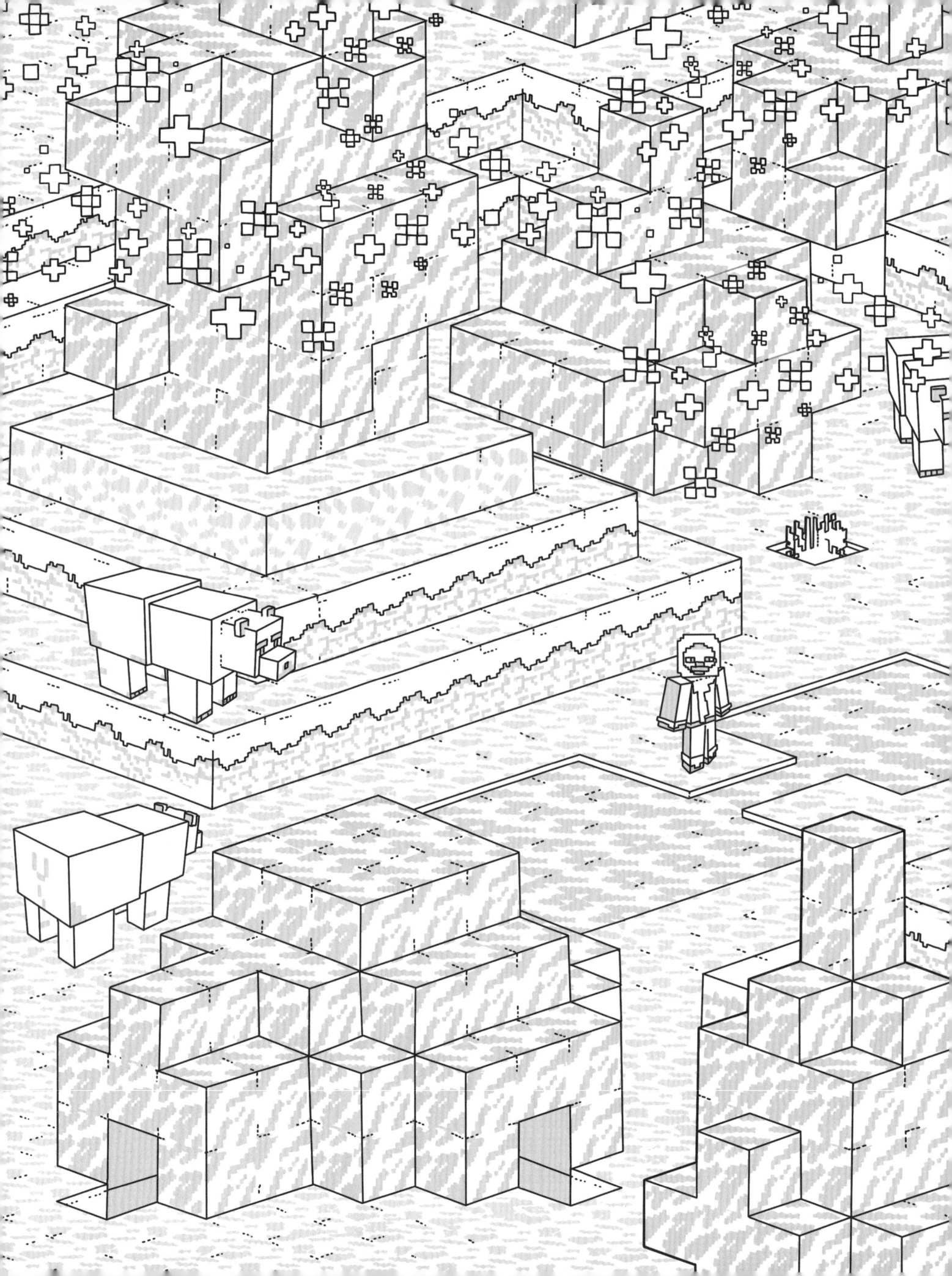

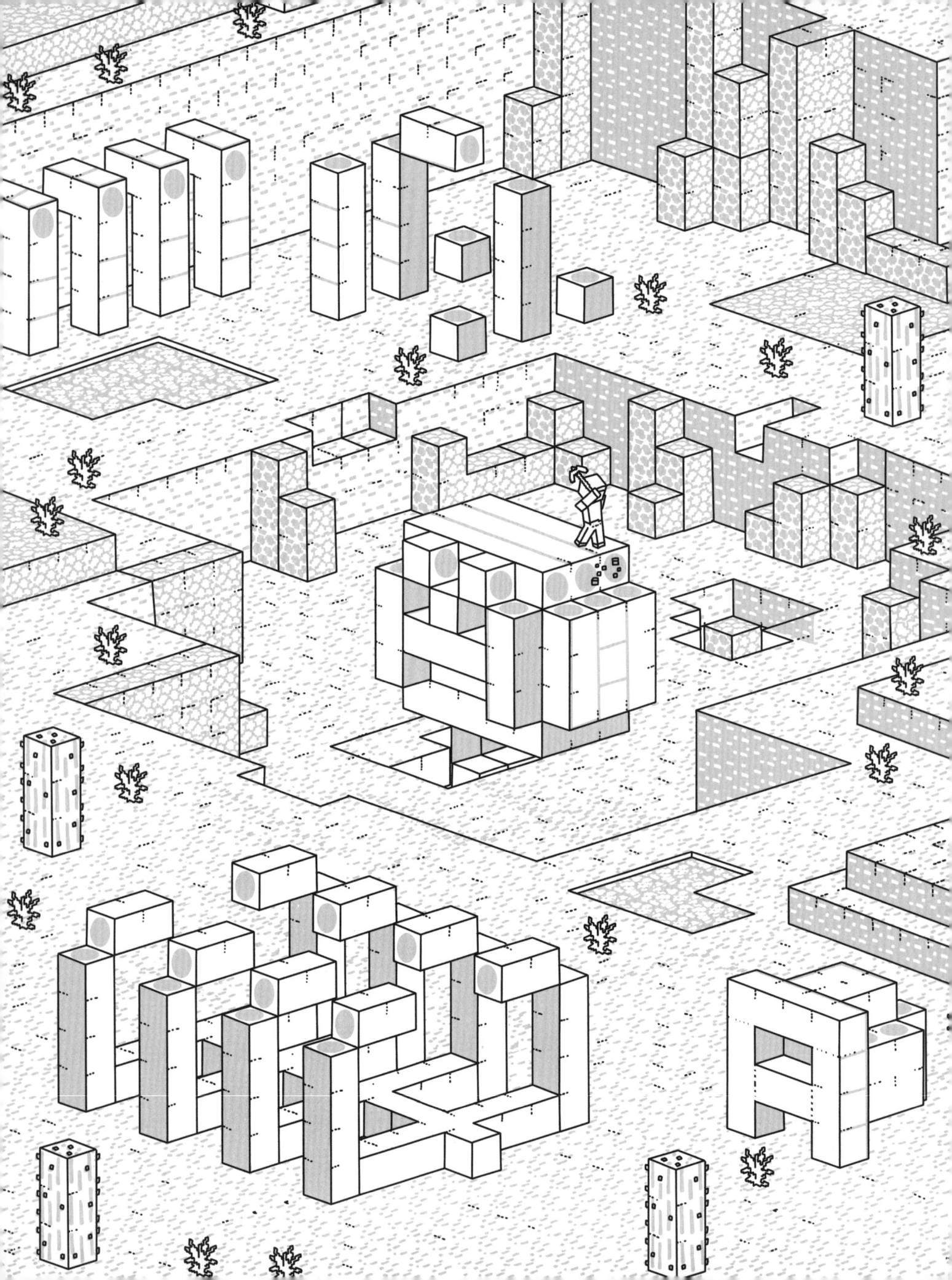

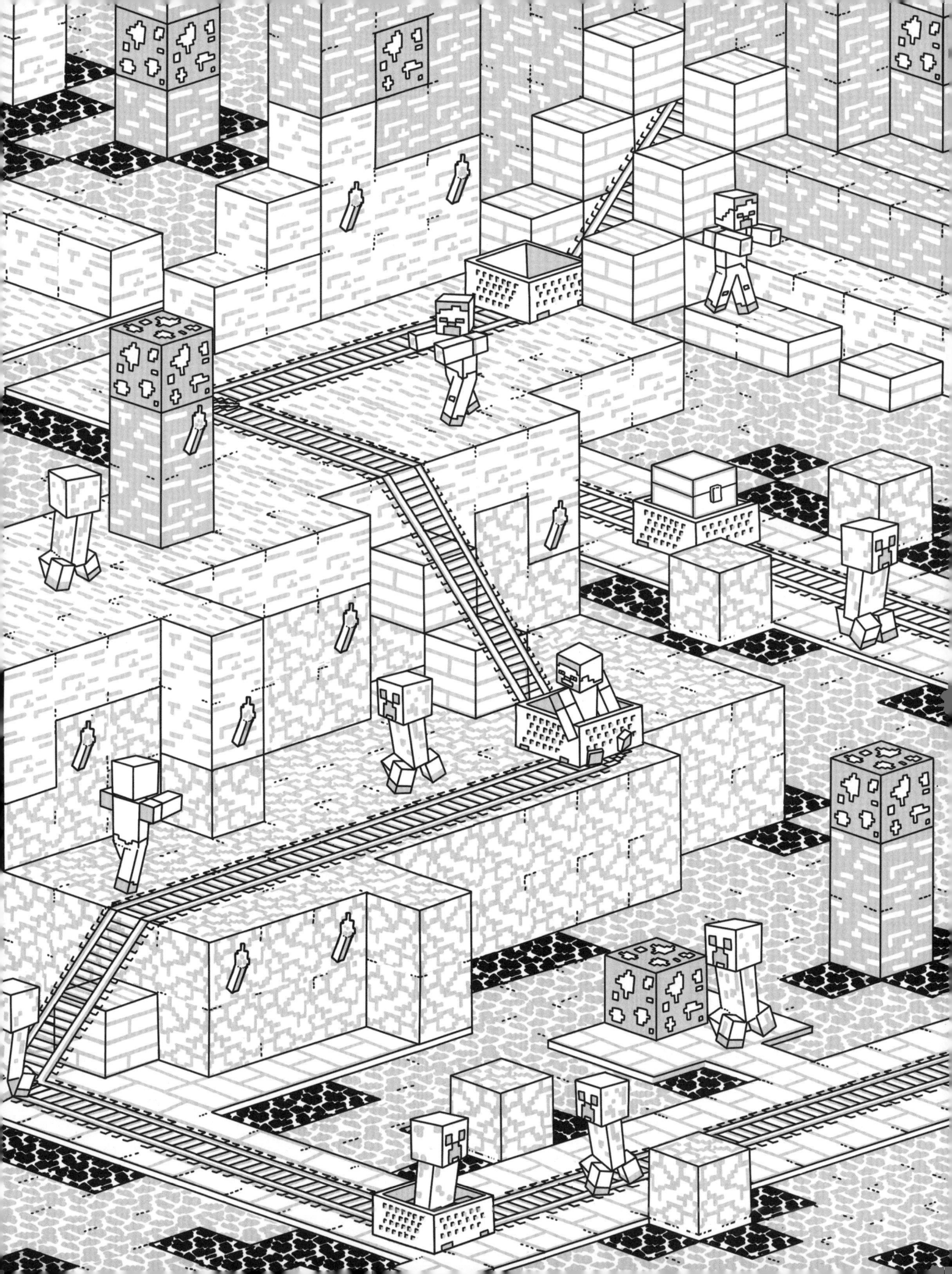

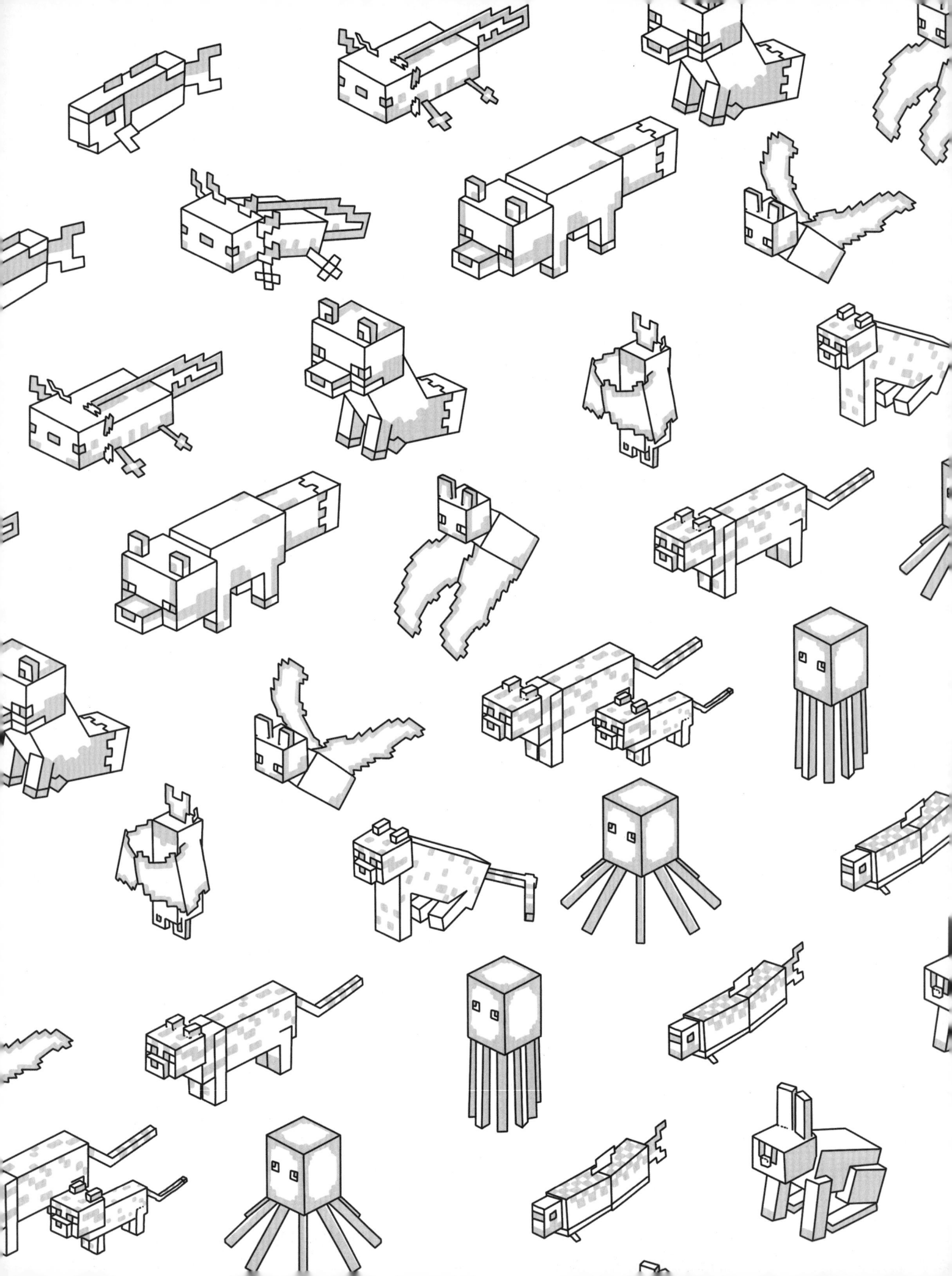

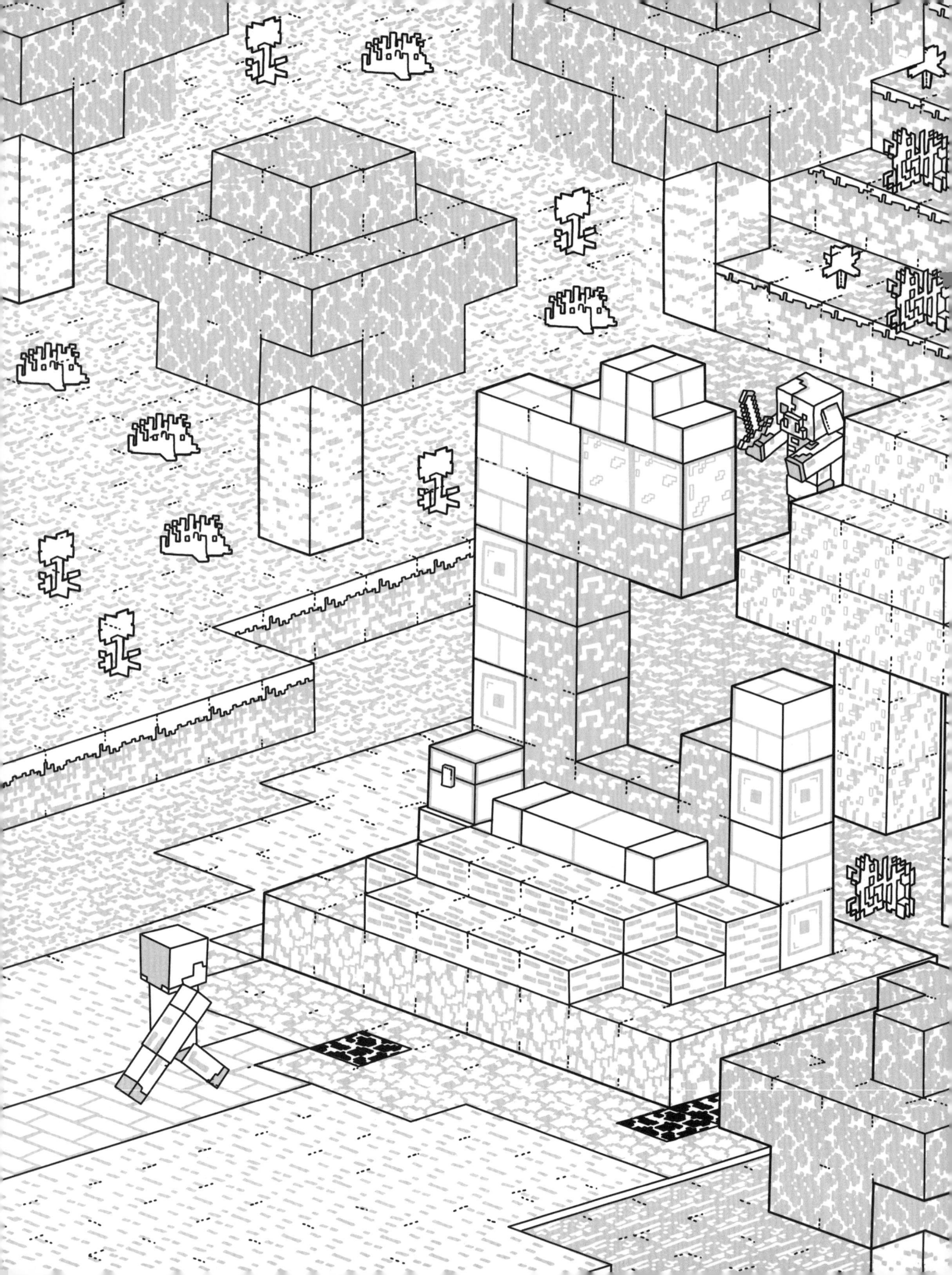

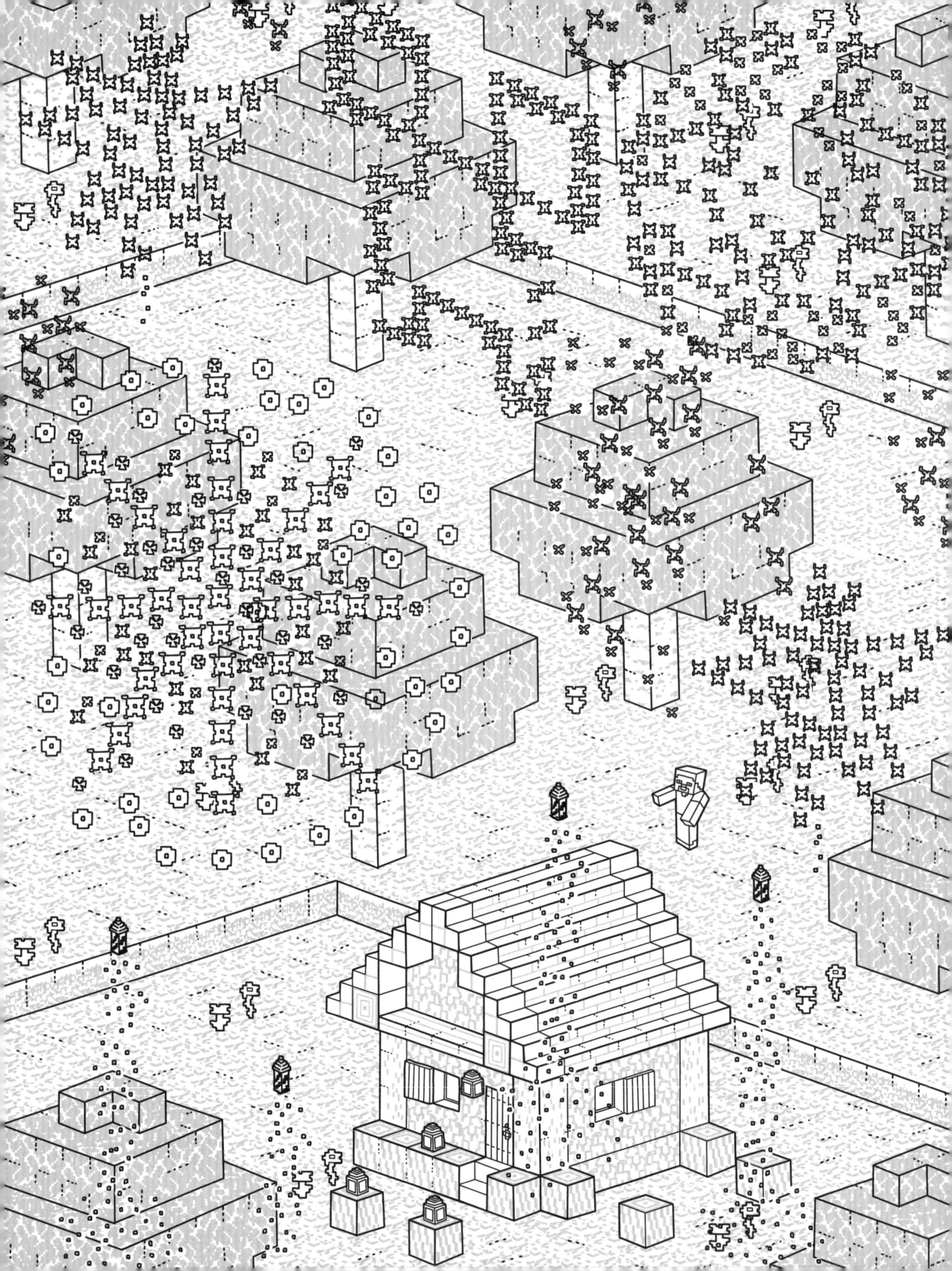

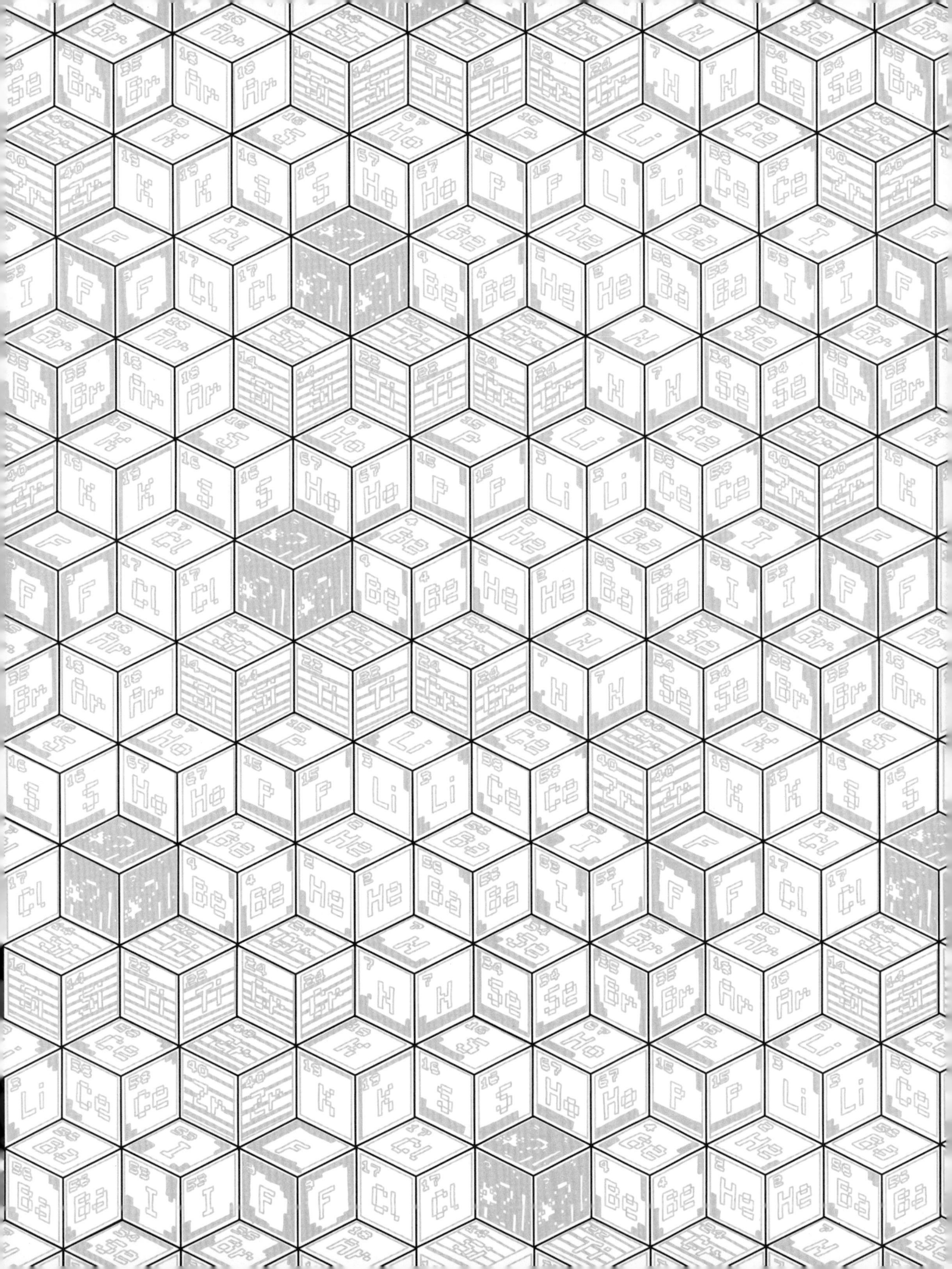

TITAN BOOKS

Published by Titan Books, London, in 2022
A division of Titan Publishing Group Ltd
144 Southwark Street
London SE1 0UP
www.titanbooks.com

Find us on Facebook: facebook.com/TitanBooks
Follow us on X: @TitanBooks

No part of this publication may be reproduced, stored in a retrieval system, or transmitted, in any form or by any means without the prior written permission of the publisher, nor be otherwise circulated in any form of binding or cover other than that in which it is published and without a similar condition being imposed on the subsequent purchase.

A CIP catalogue record for this title is available from the British Library.
EU RP (for authorities only)
eucomply OÜ Pärnu mnt 139b-14 11317 Talinn, Estonia
hello@eucompliancepartner.com, +3375690241

ISBN: 978-1-80336-386-8

© 2022 Mojang AB. All Rights Reserved. Minecraft, the Minecraft logo, the Mojang Studios logo and the Creeper logo are trademarks of the Microsoft group of companies.

Published in the US by Insight Editions, San Rafael, California, in 2022.

Publisher: Raoul Goff
VP of Licensing and Partnerships: Vanessa Lopez
VP of Creative: Chrissy Kwasnik
VP of Manufacturing: Alix Nicholaeff
VP, Editorial Director: Vicki Jaeger
Publishing Director: Mike Degler
Design Manager: Megan Sinead Harris
Designer: Brooke McCullum
Editor: Anna Wostenberg
Managing Editor: Maria Spano
Senior Production Editor: Katie Rokakis

Production Associate: Kevin G. Yuen
Senior Production Planner: Lina s Palma-Temena

Illustrated by Valentin Ramon
Minecraft Master Builder: Christian Glücklich

Hey Minecraft Community!
Make sure to look for
MINECRAFT: GATHER, COOK, EAT! OFFICIAL COOKBOOK.
Available in stores and online.

Roots of Peace REPLANTED PAPER

Special THANK YOU to Sherin Kwan, Alex Wiltshire, Audrey Searcy, and the Mojang Team

Insight Editions, in association with Roots of Peace, will plant two trees for each tree used in the manufacturing of this book. Roots of Peace is an internationally renowned humanitarian organization dedicated to eradicating land mines worldwide and converting war-torn lands into productive farms and wildlife habitats. Roots of Peace will plant two million fruit and nut trees in Afghanistan and provide farmers there with the skills and support necessary for sustainable land use.

Manufactured in China by Insight Editions

10 9 8 7 6 5 4 3 2